HELLO ORIGAMI

30 FUN & EASY Origami Designs
for Secret Notes & Special Messages

Mizutama

INTRODUCTION

Remember when you would write a note during class, then fold it up before passing it to your best friend? Inspired by this nostalgic memory, I have created a collection of fun and easy origami designs perfect for sending secret notes and special messages.

Transform you notes into simple geometric shapes like stars, hearts, or envelopes using just a few basic folds. Or learn how to fold a cupcake, present, or bow perfect for cards, gift tags, and decorations to celebrate the special moments in life. There are even some bookmark and paperclip projects to help you stay organized at work or school.

The best thing about these designs is that they don't require fancy paper or expensive art supplies. You can use common office supplies you already have on hand, like notebook paper and even sticky notes! My favorite part of the process is using markers, highlighters, and tape to add fun doodles and messages. Check out the Inspiration Gallery at the back of the book for ideas on how to personalize and embellish your notes.

I hope you enjoy these fun and festive projects and are inspired to try your hand at a few—I guarantee they will brighten anyone's day!

MIZUTAMA

CONTENTS

TOOLS & MATERIALS

PAPER

You can use just about any type of paper to make your own origami notes. When selecting your paper, consider color, pattern, and texture. The following guide includes some of my favorite papers to use for origami notes.

ORIGAMI PAPER

There are so many different styles of origami paper on the market today. Look for paper in colors and patterns that coordinate with the finished design of your project. Use double-sided origami paper for projects in which the front and back will be visible.

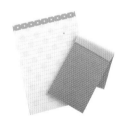

NOTEPADS

It's easy to find cute and colorful notepads in stationery shops and chain stores. Just remember, you may need to trim the paper down to size before you start folding.

NOTEBOOK & LOOSE LEAF PAPER

Lined writing paper works well for designs with a lot of text.

STICKY NOTES

With a little patience, these bright little pieces of paper make adorable origami notes. You can use both the square and rectangular versions.

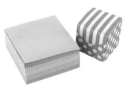

NOTE BLOCKS

These convenient notepads that commonly reside on desks make excellent origami paper because they are already square.

OTHER SUPPLIES

You don't need a lot of fancy art supplies to make origami notes. Here are a few of my favorite tools and materials for decorating notes.

BALLPOINT PENS

These pens are perfect for writing messages and doodling illustrations. You can buy ballpoint pens in a variety of colors, or buy a mutlicolor pen that contains several different shades of ink.

WASHI TAPE

This thin masking tape is available in many different colors, patterns, and sizes. Use it to decorate your notes.

MARKERS

Markers are a great option when you need to cover a large area or draw a thick line. I recommend dual-tipped markers with thick and thin nibs.

WHITE PEN

A white gel pen is a handy way to decorate dark paper. The white ink really pops off the page!

STRING

Use colorful string or yarn to attach your origami note to a gift or string several designs together to form a garland.

STICKERS

Use stickers to seal and decorate your origami notes. Circular stickers designed to be used for price tags are inexpensive and are readily available at office supply stores.

MIZUTAMA'S FAVORITE TOOLS

ERASABLE HIGHLIGHTERS

Erasable highlighters are great for drawing patterned borders. Just draw your design, then erase segments to create a border that utilizes both positive and negative space.

Erase dashes, dots, or entire lines for a unique border

Try FriXion Light highlighters from Pilot

REMOVABLE ADHESIVE

Removable adhesive pens can transform any paper into a sticky note. Just apply the glue, then let it dry to form a tacky surface.

Make any paper into a sticky note

Try the Mindwave brand Stick Marker from Japan or Scotch brand Removable Restickable Glue Stick.

STAPLELESS STAPLER

Stapleless staplers are an eco-friendly way to attach sheets of paper (metal staples prevent paper from being recyclable).

Try the Kokuyo Harinacs stapleless stapler

Add a message like "OPEN HERE" so the recipient will know to look inside

CORRECTION TAPE AND FLUID

Don't worry if you can't get your hands on fancy origami paper . . . you can make your own using solid-colored paper and correction tape or fluid. Use the tape to create linear patterns and the fluid for dots.

FOLDING BASICS

All of the projects in this book are made with basic origami folds. The following guide explains how to make these simple folds and shows the symbols commonly used to represent these techniques.

Let's get started!

VALLEY FOLD

Fold so the crease is at the bottom

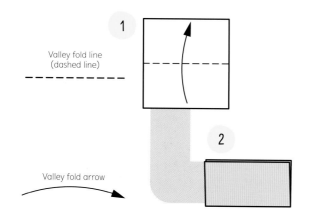

Valley fold line
(dashed line)

Valley fold arrow

MOUNTAIN FOLD

Fold so the crease is at the top

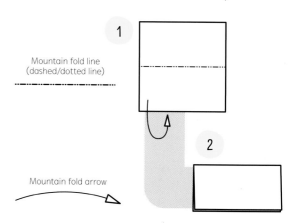

Mountain fold line
(dashed/dotted line)

Mountain fold arrow

DIVIDE EQUALLY

Divide into equally sized sections

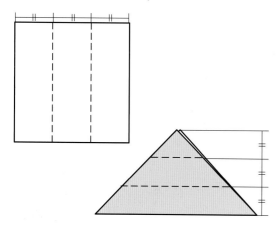

CREASE

Fold, then unfold

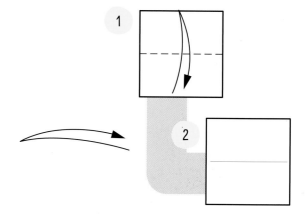

ENLARGE

The next diagram has been enlarged

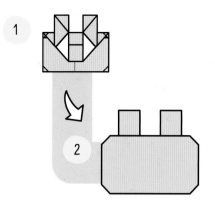

SQUASH FOLD

Insert your finger at the white arrow, open the layers, and flatten

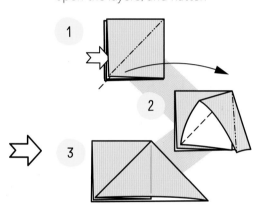

PLEAT FOLD

Make a valley fold, then a mountain fold

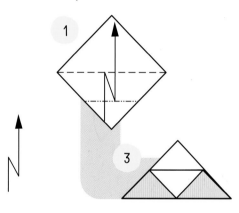

INSIDE REVERSE FOLD

Fold inside along the fold line indicated

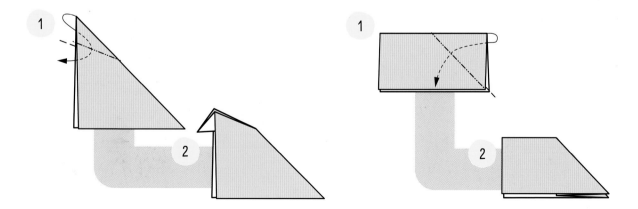

HEARTS

This sweet design is perfect for sending love notes! Any type of rectangular paper will work well for this project.

PAPER Shape: Rectangle **Size:** 3 ¼ x 4 ¾in (8.5 x 12cm) for small heart and 4 ¼ x 5 ¾in (10.5 x 14.5cm) for large heart

HOW TO MAKE

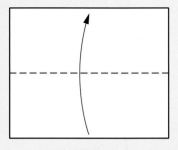

1. Fold in half.

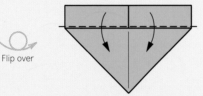

2. Fold in half and unfold.

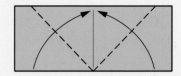
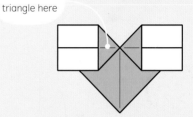

3. Fold the bottom corners to the center line.

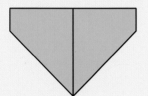

4. The bottom now forms a point.

Flip over

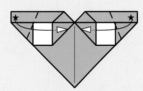

5. Fold the top edges down along the dotted line.

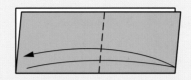

Fold into triangle here

6. On each side, open the top section to separate the two layers and flatten into a triangle at the center (squash fold).

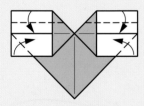

7. Fold along the dotted lines.

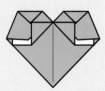

8. Insert the areas marked with ★s into the flaps at the center.

9. Completed view of step 8.

Flip over

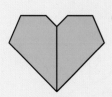

10. The heart is complete.

STARS

These sweet little stars make adorable notes or decorations. Try using metallic origami paper or wrapping paper for a dazzling effect!

PAPER Shape: Square Size: 3 x 3in (7.5 x 7.5cm) for small star and 4 ¾ x 4 ¾in (11.8 x 11.8cm) for large star

HOW TO MAKE

Start!

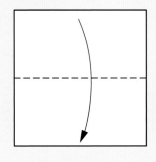

1. Fold in half.

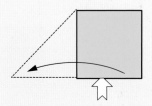

2. Fold in half again.

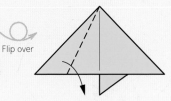

3. Open the top layer of paper only and flatten into a triangle (squash fold).

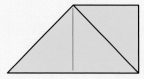

4. Flip over and repeat step 3 on the other side.

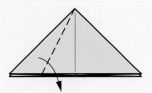

5. Fold the top section along the dotted line, bringing it to the center line.

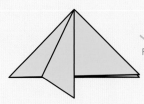

6. Completed view of step 5.

Flip over

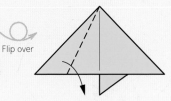

7. Repeat step 5.

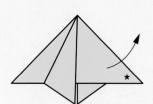

8. Hold the paper at the ★ and pull up to unfold until the work looks like the step 9 picture.

9. Completed view of step 8.

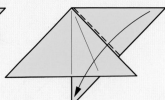

10. Fold down to align with the bottom point.

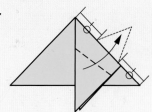

11. Fold along the dotted line so the two areas marked by Os are equal.

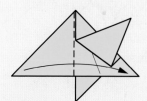

12. Fold the left side to align with the right point.

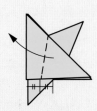

13. Fold along the dotted line.

14. Completed view of step 13.

Flip over

15. The star is complete.

DRESSES

Design your own dresses using double-sided patterned origami paper. Stripes, polka dots, and brightly-colored solids are perfectly suited for this stylish design. Don't forget to add a secret note inside!

PAPER Shape: Square **Size:** 6 x 6in (15 x 15cm)

Want to go shopping on Saturday?

Trim the paper to create different collar styles.

HOW TO MAKE

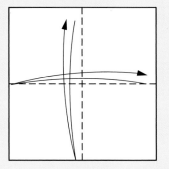 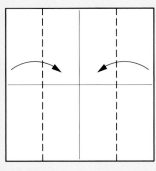 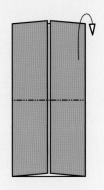 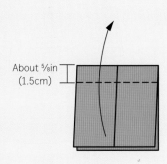

1. Fold the paper in half and unfold. Then fold the paper in half in the opposite direction and unfold. The paper is now creased into four equal sections.

2. Fold the left and right edges to the center.

3. Fold in half toward the back.

4. Fold the top half up about ⅝in (1.5cm) from the fold.

About ⅝in (1.5cm)

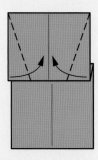 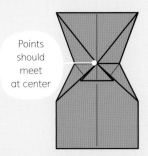 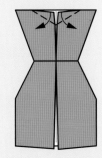 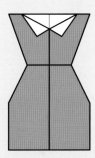

Points should meet at center

Flip over

5. Bring each corner toward the center to fold along the dotted lines.

6. Flatten the bottom into triangles where the paper naturally curls.

7. Fold along the dotted lines.

8. The collar is now complete.

 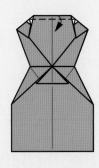 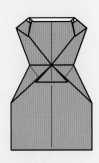 

Flip over

Flip over

9. Fold the top corners along the dotted lines.

10. Fold the top edge over slightly.

11. Completed view of step 10.

12. The dress is complete.

Good luck tomorrow!

LADYBUGS & FOUR-LEAF CLOVERS

Ladybugs and four–leaf clovers are both good luck symbols. These designs are perfect for sending well wishes to someone starting a new job or school.

PAPER (FOR BOTH) **Shape:** Square **Size:** 6 x 6in (15 x 15cm)

For a different look, fold the wings open . . . it creates the perfect spot to draw a cute little face.

HOW TO MAKE THE LADYBUGS

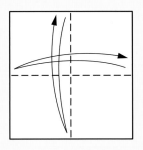
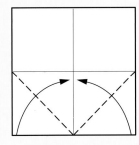
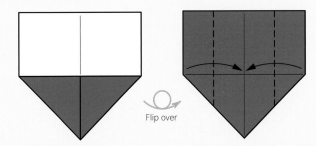

1. Fold the paper in half and unfold. Then fold the paper in half in the opposite direction and unfold. The paper is now creased into four equal sections.

2. Fold the bottom corners to the center.

3. Completed view of step 2.

4. Fold the left and right edges to the center line.

Flip over

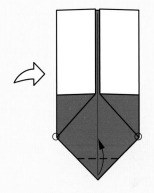
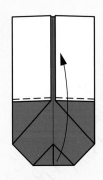
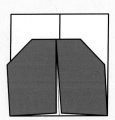
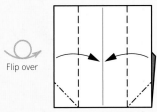

5. Fold the bottom point up so it is even with the Os.

6. Fold the bottom up along the dotted line.

7. Completed view of step 6.

8. Fold the top layers of the left and right edges to the center line. Flatten the bottom corners into triangles (squash fold).

Flip over

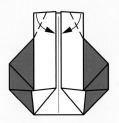
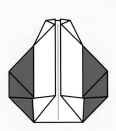
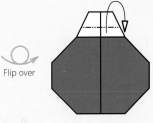
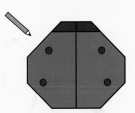

9. Fold the top corners diagonally.

10. Completed view of step 9.

11. Fold the top back.

12. Use a black marker to color the head and draw spots. The ladybug is complete.

Flip over

HOW TO MAKE THE FOUR-LEAF CLOVER

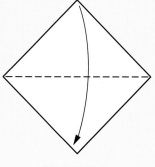

1. Fold in half

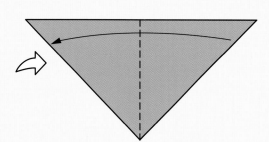

2. Fold in half again.

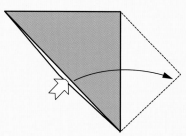

3. Open and flatten the top layer (squash fold).

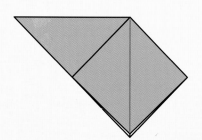

4. Flip over and repeat step 3.

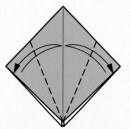

5. Fold the left and right points to the center, then unfold.

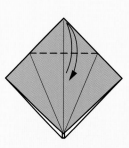

6. Fold the top point down, then unfold.

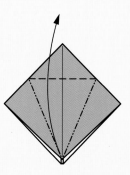

7. Open the top layer by folding it back along the crease made in step 6.

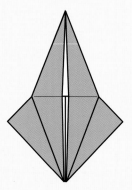

8. Fold along the step 5 creases to bring the left and right edges in to form an upper and a lower triangle. Flip over and repeat steps 7 and 8 on the other side.

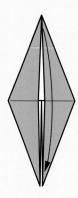

9. Fold the upper triangle down.

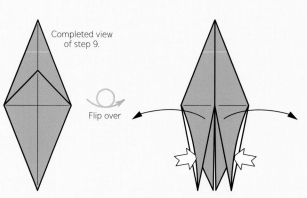

Completed view of step 9.

Flip over

10. Insert your finger between the two layers as indicated by the white arrows. On each side, bring the triangle up and flatten.

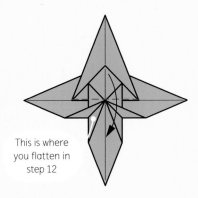

Pay attention . . . this is the tricky part!

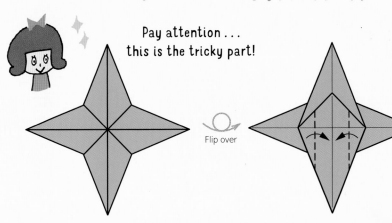

11. Completed view of step 10.

12. Fold both sides to the center line, then open and flatten the resulting triangles, as shown in step 13.

This is where you flatten in step 12

13. Fold along the red line.

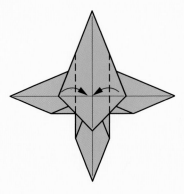

14. Repeat step 12 for the upper triangle.

This is where you flatten in step 14

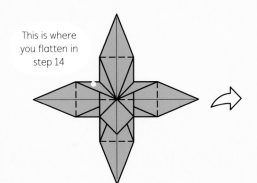

15. Fold along the dotted lines to bring the points to the center.

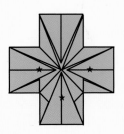

16. Tuck the points marked with ★s into the flaps underneath.

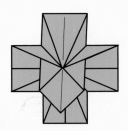

17. Completed view of step 16.

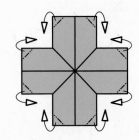

Flip over

18. Fold the corners back on each leaf.

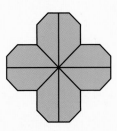

19. The four-leaf clover is complete.

SOCKS

Made from sticky notes, these miniature socks are designed for short and sweet messages . . . plus, they're fun to decorate! Fold several and string together for an adorable clothes line-inspired garland.

PAPER Shape: Square **Size:** 3 x 3in (8 x 8cm)

Sticky notes are the perfect size for these cute little socks.

Knitting class @ 6

HOW TO MAKE

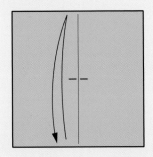 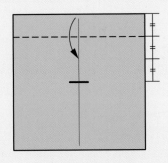 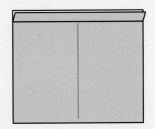

1. Fold the top down to meet the bottom edge. Press lightly to mark the center, but do not crease.

2. Visually divide the top half into three equal sections. Fold the top ⅓ down.

3. Fold the top layer back up to meet the fold.

4. Completed view of step 3.

 Flip over

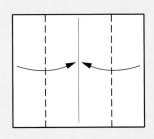 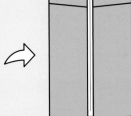 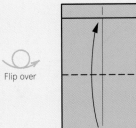 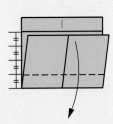

5. Fold the left and right edges to the center line.

6. Completed view of step 5.

7. Fold the bottom up to meet the upper fold.

8. Fold back down along the dotted line.

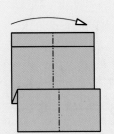 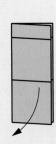 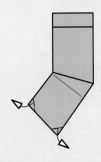 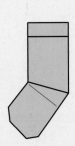

9. Mountain fold in half.

10. Pull the bottom of the sock down diagonally as shown in step 11.

11. Fold the corners back.

12. The sock is complete.

DONUTS

This sweet donut features the perfect spot for drawing a little doodle or jotting a quick note. It makes a great birthday card or note to accompany homemade baked goods.

PAPER **Shape:** Square **Size:** 6 x 6in (15 x 15cm)

HOW TO MAKE

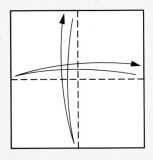

1. Fold the paper in half and unfold. Then fold the paper in half in the opposite direction and unfold. The paper is now creased into four equal sections.

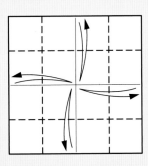

2. Fold each edge to the center, then unfold. The paper is now creased into sixteen equal sections.

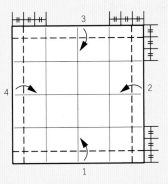

3. Following the numerical order shown above, fold each edge in ⅓ of the way to the first grid line.

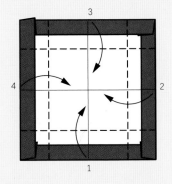

4. Following the numerical order shown above, fold each edge in along the crease lines from step 2.

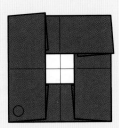

5. Unfold the left edge (marked by O), then refold so that the left edge is tucked underneath the bottom edge, as shown in step 6.

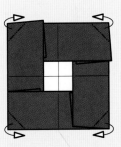

6. Fold the corners back.

7. The donut is complete.

TWO-TONED DONUT

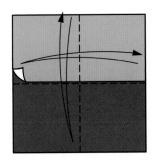 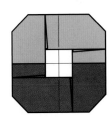

Cut a sheet of 6 x 6in (15 x 15cm) origami paper in half and align it on top of a full-size sheet of origami paper in another color. Follow steps 1-7 listed above to complete the donut.

ENVELOPE

Use a few basic folds to turn your top secret note into an envelope. You could also write a note on a small scrap of paper and insert it into this handmade envelope.

PAPER **Shape:** Rectangle **Size:** About 5 x 6 ¾in (12.5 x 17cm)

HOW TO MAKE

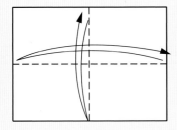

1. Fold the paper in half and unfold. Then fold the paper in half in the opposite direction and unfold. The paper is now creased into four equal sections.

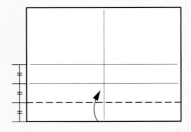

2. Measure and divide the bottom half of the paper into three equal sections. Fold the bottom ⅓ up.

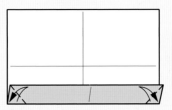

3. Fold and unfold the bottom corners to crease at an angle.

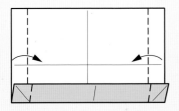

4. Fold the left and right edges in using the crease from step 3 as a guide.

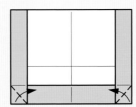

5. Fold the bottom corners up again along the crease from step 3.

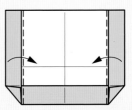

6. Fold the left and right edges in again.

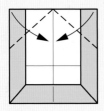

7. Fold the top corners to the center line.

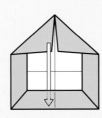

8. Insert the top triangle into the bottom flap.

Seal with a sticker!

9. The envelope is complete.

BOWS

Send a pretty bow-inspired noted to your favorite girly girl.

PAPER Shape: Rectangle
Size: 3 x 5in (7.5 x 12.5cm) for small bow or 4 x 6in (10 x 15cm) for large bow

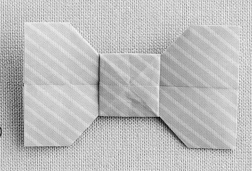

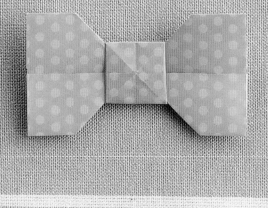

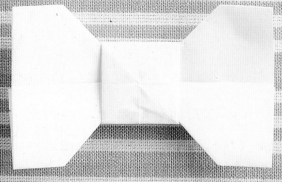

HOW TO MAKE

I love wearing bows in my hair!

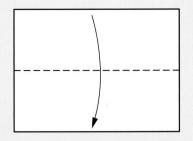

1. Fold in half. Crease, then unfold.

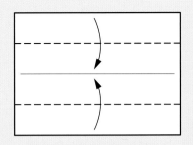

2. Fold the top and bottom edges to the center line.

3. Fold in half.

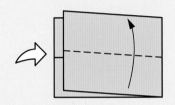

4. Fold in half again.

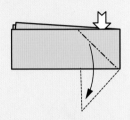

5. Open the top layer and flatten into a triangle (squash fold).

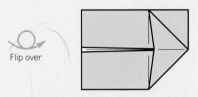

Flip over

6. Repeat step 5 on the other side.

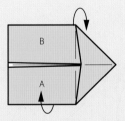

7. Fold rectangle A up so it is on top of rectangle B. Fold the rectangle hidden underneath B down.

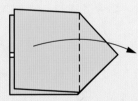

8. Fold the top layer along the dotted line.

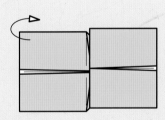

9. Fold the left half back.

10. Fold the left corners in to the center line. Without flipping the work over, repeat on the other side.

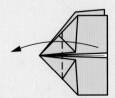

11. Fold the top layer along the dotted line. Bring the right edge over the left and flatten the center into a square.

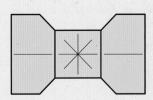

12. The bow is complete.

LITTLE BIRD GIFT TAG

You can use this little birdie as a cute note, or add some string and attach it to a gift. The wing makes an excellent spot for personalizing the tag with a special message.

PAPER Shape: Square **Size:** 6 x 6in (15 x 15cm)

FLOWER CLIPS

Sign these forms by Monday!

These sweet little blooms are made using the same folding process as the four-leaf clover on page 16—just use brightly colored paper and embellish with a circular sticker to transform into a flower. Attach a paper clip to the back to turn these pretty posies into practical office supplies.

PAPER Shape: Square **Size:** 3 x 3in (7.5 x 7.5cm)

HOW TO MAKE THE LiTTLE BiRD GiFT TAG

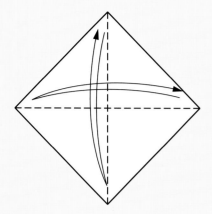

1. Fold the paper in half and unfold. Then fold the paper in half in the opposite direction and unfold. The paper is now creased into four equal sections.

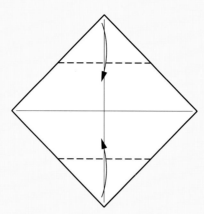

2. Fold the top and bottom points to the center.

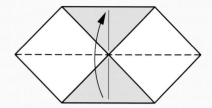

3. Fold in half.

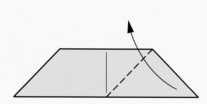

4. Fold the right point diagonally.

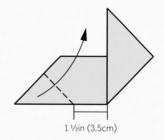

1 ½in (3.5cm)

5. Fold the left point diagonally so that there is about 1 ½in (3.5cm) of space in the middle.

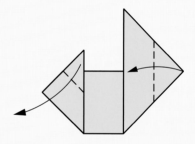

6. Fold along the dotted lines.

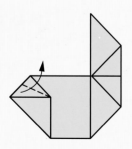

7. Fold along the dotted line.

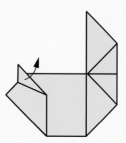

8. Turn the triangle marked by the arrow over so it faces the opposite direction, as shown in step 9.

Fold so the tip extends ¼in (5mm)

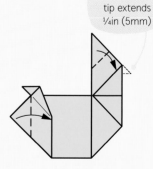

9. Fold along the dotted lines.

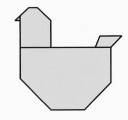

Wing Template

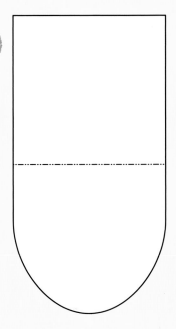

10. Fold the top point down slightly.

Flip over

11. Completed view of step 10.

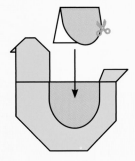

12. Use the template to cut a wing out of a separate sheet of paper. Tuck the wing in between the two layers of the body.

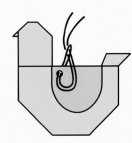

13. Make a hole and insert the string.

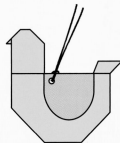

14. The bird is complete.

HOW TO MAKE THE FLOWER CLIPS

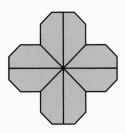

1. Follow steps 1–19 to make the Four-Leaf Clover as shown on pages 18–19.

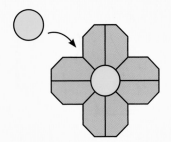

2. Adhere a circular sticker to the center.

This part should hang over the wrong side of the paper.

3. Clip the flower to a sheet of paper to use it as a bookmark. Or try gluing a paper clip to the wrong side of the flower.

FLOWERS

These pretty blooms contain the perfect spot for jotting down a quick note or greeting. Use patterned origami paper or decorate solid paper with fun designs.

PAPER **Shape:** Square **Size:** Two 3 x 3in (7.5 x 7.5cm) sheets

HOW TO MAKE THE PETALS

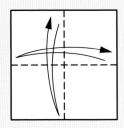

1. Fold the paper in half and unfold. Then fold the paper in half in the opposite direction and unfold. The paper is now creased into four equal sections.

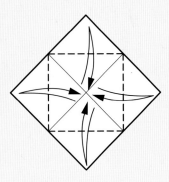

2. Rotate the paper so it is positioned like a diamond. Fold each point to the center, then unfold.

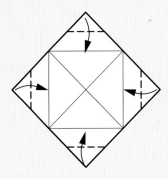

3. Fold each point to the crease lines created in step 2.

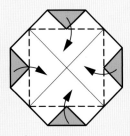

4. Fold in along the crease lines created in step 2.

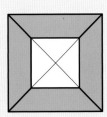

5. Completed view of step 4.

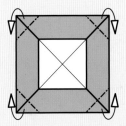

6. Fold the corners back.

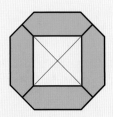

7. The petals are complete.

HOW TO MAKE THE STEM

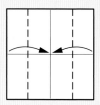

1. Complete step 1 as shown above for the flower. Next, fold the left and right edges to the center line.

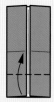

2. Fold the bottom edge to the center line.

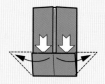

3. Pull out the bottom layers and flatten into triangles (squash fold).

4. Fold the right edge along the dotted line.

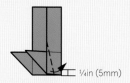
¼in (5mm)

5. Fold the top triangle diagonally along the dotted line.

6. Bring the left edge over the right, folding the stem in half.

7. Fold the top triangle diagonally along the dotted line.

8. Completed view of step 7.

Flip over

9. The stem is complete.

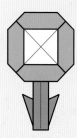

10. Glue the stem to the back of the petals to complete the flower.

LITTLE RED RIDING HOOD PUPPET SHOW

This adorable Little Red Riding Hood puppet is a fun way to brighten a child's day. Don't forget the forest scenery—fold trees, then embellish with drawings of leaves, fruit, or nuts.

PAPER FOR TREE **Shape:** Square **Size:** Two 4 ¾ x 4 ¾in (11.8 x 11.8cm) sheets

PAPER FOR LITTLE RED RIDING HOOD **Shape:** Square **Size:** 6 x 6in (15 x 15cm)

HOW TO MAKE THE TREE TOP

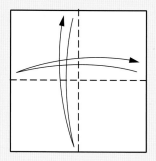

1. Fold the paper in half and unfold. Then fold the paper in half in the opposite direction and unfold. The paper is now creased into four equal sections.

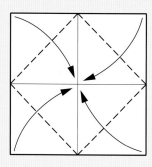

2. Fold the corners to the center.

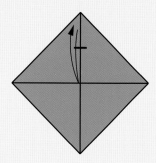

3. Fold the top point to the center and unfold. Draw a line to mark the resulting crease.

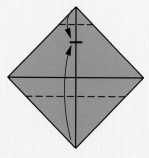

4. Fold the top and bottom points to the line made in step 3.

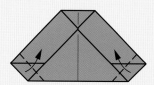

5. Fold the corners diagonally.

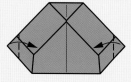

6. Fold the left and right points in.

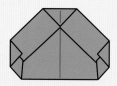

7. Completed view of step 6.

Flip over

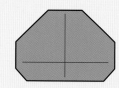

8. The tree top is complete.

HOW TO MAKE THE TRUNK

GETTING STARTED

Fold the paper into ninths, then cut out one square to use for the trunk.

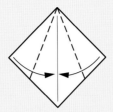

1. Fold the left and right points to the center line.

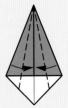

2. Fold the left and right edges to the center line again.

3. Fold the bottom up.

4. Completed view of step 3.

Flip over

5. The trunk is complete.

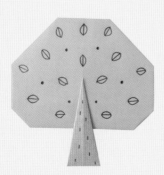

6. Glue the trunk to the tree top.

HOW TO MAKE LITTLE RED RIDING HOOD

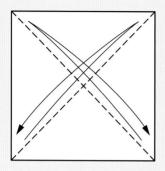

1. Fold the paper in half and unfold. Then fold the paper in half in the opposite direction and unfold. The paper is now creased into four equal sections.

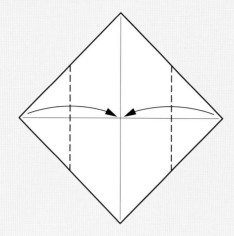

2. Fold the left and right points to the center line.

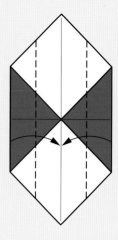

3. Fold the left and right edges to the center line again.

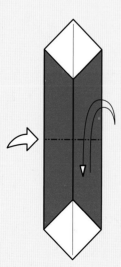

4. Mountain fold in half, then unfold.

Valley fold

Mountain fold from step 4

5. Valley fold along the dotted line to complete the pleat fold.

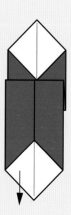

6. Pull the bottom to unfold.

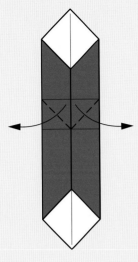

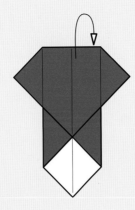

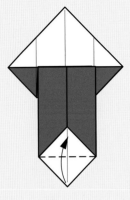

7. Fold along the dotted lines, then bring the top down and flatten (squash fold).

8. Fold the top backward, causing a white triangle to appear as shown in step 9.

9. Fold the bottom up.

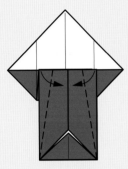

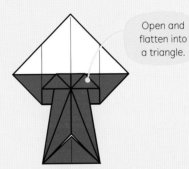

Open and flatten into a triangle.

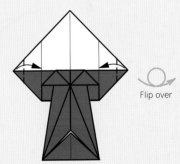

Flip over

10. Fold the top corners of the rectangle diagonally, bringing them to the center line.

11. Open the points and flatten into triangles (squash fold).

12. Fold the left and right corners in.

Face Template

13. Draw a face on a separate sheet of paper, then cut it out.

14. Glue the face to the body to complete Little Red Riding Hood.

Use this template or draw your own!

BUTTERFLIES

These colorful butterflies feature special loops on the back, allowing you to wear the design as a ring or use it to hold a rolled note.

PAPER Shape: Square **Size:** 6 x 6in (15 x 15cm)

HOW TO MAKE

GETTING STARTED

Cut a sheet of origami paper in half before you start folding.

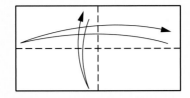

1. Fold the paper in half and unfold. Then fold the paper in half in the opposite direction and unfold. The paper is now creased into four equal sections.

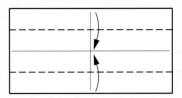

2. Fold the top and bottom edges to the center line.

3. Fold the left and right edges to the center line.

4. Completed view of step 3.

Flip over

5. Fold the top layers only to the center line. Squash fold to flatten the corners into triangles.

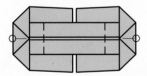

6. Crease along the dotted lines. Bring the wings (marked by Os) to the front.

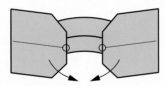

7. Position the wings like this.

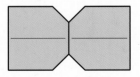

8. Completed view of step 7.

Some of the tape should stick out on the top

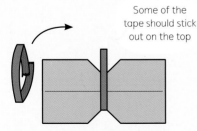

9. Bring the wings together. Use a looped piece of washi tape to hold them together.

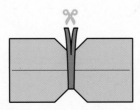

10. Make a clip down the center of the washi tape to form the antennae.

The loop on the back allows you to wear the butterfly as a ring or use it to hold a rolled note.

STRAWBERRIES

These sweet strawberry notes are guaranteed to bring a smile to a friend's face. Use washi tape to decorate the stems and embellish with fun doodles.

PAPER Shape: Square **Size:** 3 x 3in (7.5 x 7.5cm) for small strawberry and 3 ½ x 3 ½in (8.5 x 8.5cm) for large strawberry

HOW TO MAKE

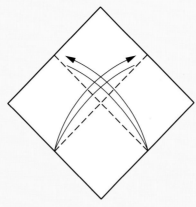

1. Fold the paper in half and unfold. Then fold the paper in half in the opposite direction and unfold. The paper is now creased into four equal sections.

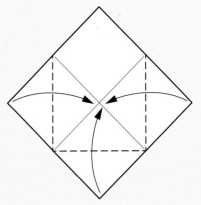

2. Fold three of the points to the center.

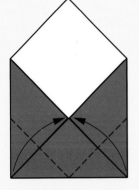

3. Fold the bottom corners to the center.

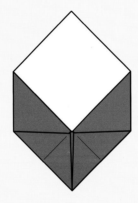

4. Completed view of step 3. The bottom now forms a point.

Flip over

5. Fold the top point down along the dotted line.

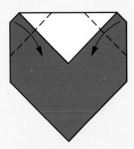

6. Fold the top corners along the dotted lines.

7. The strawberry is complete.

Add more washi tape if necessary.

SANTA AND WREATH

These designs make quick and easy holiday decorations, cards, and gift tags. They're sure to get you in the holiday spirit!

PAPER (FOR BOTH) **Shape:** Square **Size:** 6 x 6in (15 x 15cm)

Create using the same folding method as Little Red Riding Hood (page 35) and the Donut (page 22)!

MERRY CHRISTMAS!

HOW TO MAKE SANTA

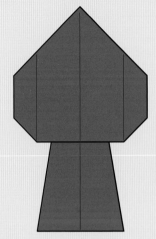

Cut it out

Draw a face

Adhere two circular stickers together with the tip of the hat sandwiched in between.

1. Follow steps 1–12 to make Little Red Riding Hood as shown on pages 38–39.

2. Draw a face on a separate sheet of paper, then cut it out.

3. Glue the face to the head, then adhere circular stickers to the hat to complete Santa.

HOW TO MAKE THE WREATH

Time to decorate!

Face Template

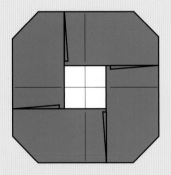

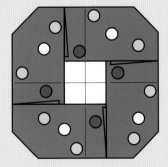

1. Follow steps 1–7 to make the Donut as shown on page 23.

2. Decorate the wreath with circular stickers.

Use this template or draw your own!

GifT TaGS

Never buy a gift tag again! Learn how to fold your own with just a few simple steps.

PAPER Shape: Rectangle **Size:** 4 ¼ x 6in (11 x 15cm), 3 ½ x 9 ¾in (9 x 25cm), or 6 x 8 ¼in (15 x 21cm)

Write a message on the inside of the tag

HOW TO MAKE

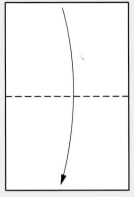

1. Fold in half.

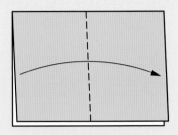

2. Fold in half again.

3. Fold the top corners diagonally.

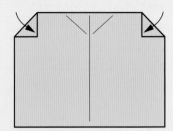

4. Open, then fold the top corners in along the crease lines from step 3.

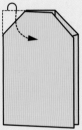

5. Close, then push the top left corner in (inside reverse fold).

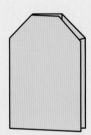

6. Completed view of step 5.

Circular sticker

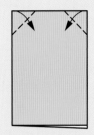

7. Adhere a circular sticker to the right side of the tag.

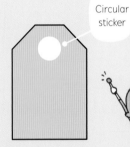

Time to add a sticker!

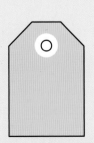

8. Punch a hole through the sticker and all layers of paper.

9. Insert a string through the hole to complete the tag.

Use brightly colored stickers and string for a festive look. You can even coordinate the tag with the color of your gift wrap.

MATRYOSHKA DOLLS

These adorable matryoshka dolls make cute little lunch box notes.
Fold a few using different sizes of paper for the classic nesting doll look.

PAPER **Shape:** Square **Size:** 3 x 3in (7.5 x 7.5cm) for small,
4 ¾ x 4 ¾in (11.8 x 11.8cm) for medium, and 6 x 6in (15 x 15cm) for large

Have a great day!

Add a stem and leaf for an apple-themed matryoshka.

Slip a mini note inside the special pocket!

Thank you

HOW TO MAKE

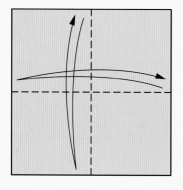

1. Fold the paper in half and unfold. Then fold the paper in half in the opposite direction and unfold. The paper is now creased into four equal sections.

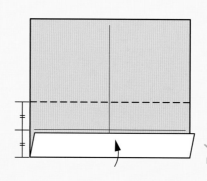

2. Visually divide the bottom half into three equal sections. Fold the bottom ⅓ up.

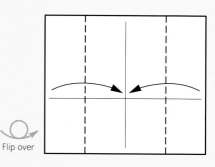

3. Fold the left and right edges to the center line.

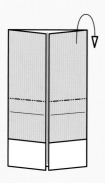

4. Mountain fold so the back is longer than the front.

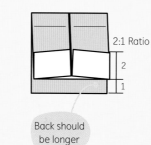

2:1 Ratio

Back should be longer

5. Completed view of step 4.

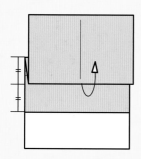

6. Fold the top layer up.

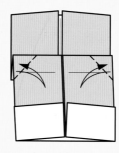

7. Fold the corners along the dotted lines, then unfold.

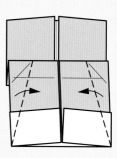

8. Fold along the dotted lines, which extend from the bottom corners to the points of the triangles creased in step 7.

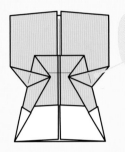

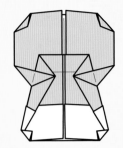

Flatten this part into a triangle

9. Open and flatten the corners of the face into triangles.

10. Fold the corners back on the head and body.

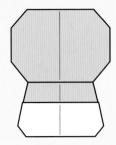

Flip over

11. Completed view of step 10.

12. Draw a face on a separate sheet of paper, then cut it out.

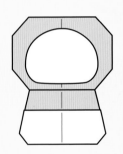

13. Glue the face to the head to complete the matryoshka.

Face Templates

Small

Medium

Large

How to Make Apple Matryoshkas

1. Cut out scraps of paper in the shape of a leaf and stem.

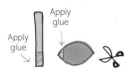

Apply glue

Apply glue

2. Apply glue as shown above. Attach the leaf to the stem, then attach the stem to the back of the matryoshka.

GIFT BOXES

Use washi tape to transform a simply folded note into a one-of-a-kind card perfect for birthdays and other special occasions. You can even enclose a gift card inside!

PAPER: Shape: Rectangle **Size:** 6 x 8in (15 x 21cm) or 4 x 6in (10 x 15cm)

HOW TO MAKE

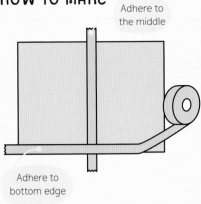

Adhere to the middle

Adhere to bottom edge

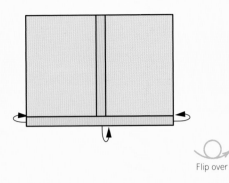

Flip over

Make sure the tape is on the outside

1. Adhere washi tape to the middle and bottom edge of the paper.

2. Fold the ends of the washi tape to the wrong side of the paper.

3. Fold the paper into thirds.

Rotate 180°

Make sure tape is in the middle

4. Fold the top and bottom edges toward the center. Insert the bottom edge between the layers of the top edge.

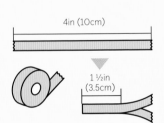

4in (10cm)

1 ½in (3.5cm)

5. To make the bow, cut a 4in (10cm) piece of washi tape. Fold it in half and adhere the two sides together for 1 ½in (3.5cm) from the fold.

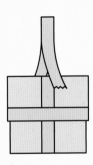

6. Adhere the washi tape to the paper.

1 ½in (3.5cm)

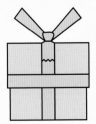

Tie together

7. Cut the washi tape in half for 1 ½in (3.5cm) from the top (stop just before the paper).

8. Tie the two ends of the tape together in a bow to complete the gift box.

Don't forget to add a message inside.

Mani pedi at
3PM on Tuesday?

Dinner at
7PM?

NAIL POLISH

These pretty nail polish notes make excellent party invitations for a girls night out. Use pastel-hued origami paper, then add metallic tape for a special touch.

PAPER Shape: Square Size: 3 x 3in (7.5 x 7.5cm)

HOW TO MAKE

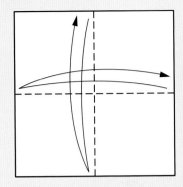

1. Fold the paper in half and unfold. Then fold the paper in half in the opposite direction and unfold. The paper is now creased into four equal sections.

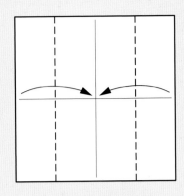

2. Fold the left and right edges to the center line.

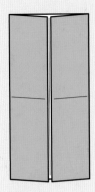

3. Completed view of step 2.

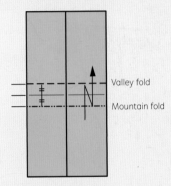

Valley fold

Mountain fold

4. Pleat fold by making a mountain fold below and a valley fold above the center line.

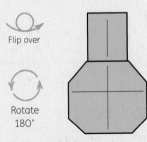

5. Fold the left and right bottom edges to the center line.

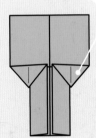

Flatten this part into a triangle

6. Open and flatten into triangles (squash fold).

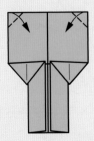

7. Fold the top corners in.

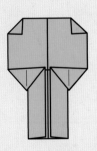

8. Completed view of step 7.

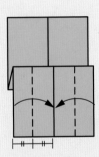

Flip over

Rotate 180°

9. View once work has been flipped over and rotated.

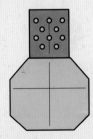

10. Adhere metallic tape to the cap section of the nail polish bottle.

PENCILS

This clever design utilizes both the right and wrong sides of the paper to form a two-tone pencil. Use this note to make planning study dates fun.

PAPER Shape: Square **Size:** 6 x 6in (15 x 15cm)

HOW TO MAKE

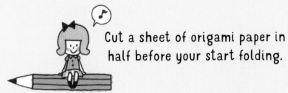

Cut a sheet of origami paper in half before your start folding.

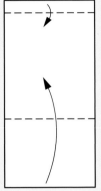

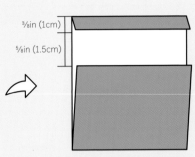

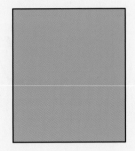

Flip over

1. Fold the top and bottom edges in along the dotted lines.

2. Completed view of step 1.

3. View once the work has been flipped over.

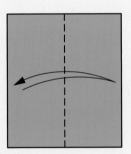

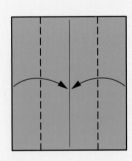

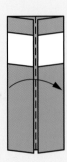

4. Fold in half. Crease, then unfold.

5. Fold the left and right edges to the center line.

6. Fold in half.

Flip over

7. Fold the top corners diagonally to form the pencil tip.

8. Completed view of step 7.

9. The pencil is complete.

CUPCAKES

These scrumptious cupcake notes make excellent birthday party invitations. Use red washi tape or a marker to decorate the cute little strawberry perched atop the frosting.

PAPER **Shape:** Square **Size:** 6 x 6in (15 x 15cm) or 7 x 7in (18 x 18cm)

HOW TO MAKE

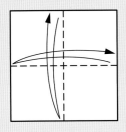

1. Fold the paper in half and unfold. Then fold the paper in half in the opposite direction and unfold. The paper is now creased into four equal sections.

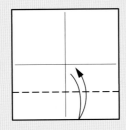

2. Fold the bottom edge to the center line, then unfold.

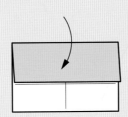

3. Fold the top edge to the crease made in step 2.

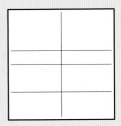

4. Unfold so the paper lies flat.

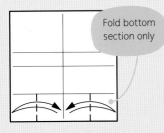

Fold bottom section only

5. For the bottom section only, fold the left and right edges to the center line, then unfold.

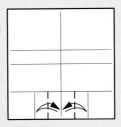

6. For the bottom section only, align the creases made in step 5 with the center line and crease.

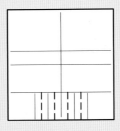

7. Follow the same process so the center squares have four creases each.

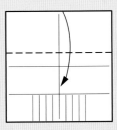

8. Fold the top edge to the first horizontal crease from the bottom (just like in step 3).

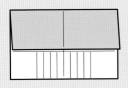

9. Completed view of step 8.

Flip over

10. Fold the left and right edges to the center line.

11. Fold the top corners diagonally.

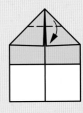

12. Fold the tip down along the dotted line.

13. Fold the bottom corners diagonally along the dotted lines.

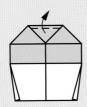

14. Fold the tip back up along the dotted line.

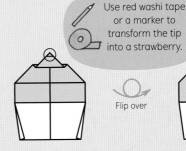

Use red washi tape or a marker to transform the tip into a strawberry.

15. Fold the tip down.

Flip over

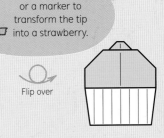

16. The cupcake is complete.

Turn upside down to transform into kids wearing party hats.

I found a new tasty ice cream shop! Let's go there together soon.

ICE CREAM CONES

A friendly ice cream note is sure to brighten anyone's day. Have fun doodling silly faces!

PAPER Shape: Square **Size:** 4 ¾ x 4 ¾in (11.8 x 11.8in) or 6 x 6in (15 x 15cm)

60

HOW TO MAKE

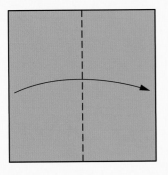

1. Fold in half. Crease, then unfold.

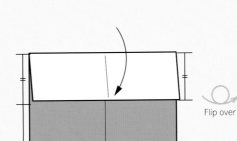

2. Fold the top ⅓ down.

Flip over

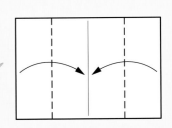

3. Fold the left and right edges to the center.

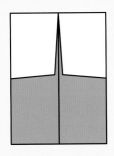

4. Completed view of step 3.

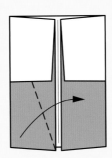

5. Fold the bottom left corner diagonally along the dotted line.

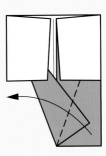

6. Fold the bottom right corner diagonally along the dotted line.

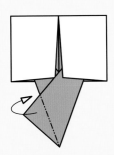

7. Fold the excess paper in.

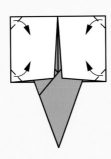

8. Fold the corners in.

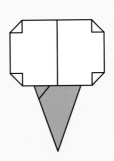

9. Completed view of step 8.

Flip over

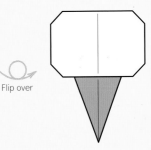

10. The ice cream cone is complete.

PANDA & BUNNY

These petite panda and bunny faces make cute little notes. The construction of the folds on the wrong side makes it possible to use this design as a bookmark or even a finger puppet!

PAPER (FOR BOTH) Shape: Square **Size:** 3 x 3in (7.5 x 7.5cm)

Glue onto a clothespin to transform this design into a clip!

HOW TO MAKE THE PANDA

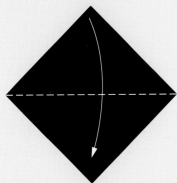

1. Fold in half, bringing the top point down to match the bottom point.

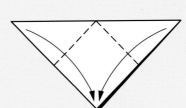

2. Fold the left and right points in to the center line.

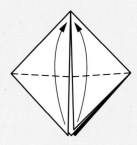

3. For the top layer only, fold in half, bringing the bottom point up to match the top point.

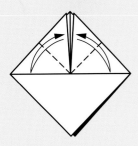

4. Fold the left and right points in to the center line. Crease, then unfold.

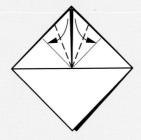

5. On each side, fold the top layer to the crease line created in step 4.

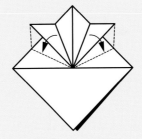

6. Open the triangles and flatten (squash fold).

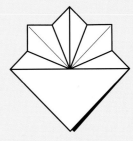

7. Completed view of step 6.

8. Fold the edges of each flattened triangle to the center line.

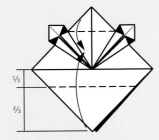

9. Fold the top and bottom points toward the center.

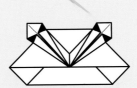

10. Insert the bottom point under the top layer as shown.

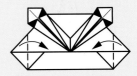

11. Fold the left and right points in.

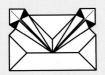

12. Completed view of step 11.

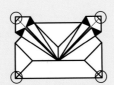

13. Fold the corners in.

14. Completed view of step 13.

Flip over

15. The panda is complete.

HOW TO MAKE THE BUNNY

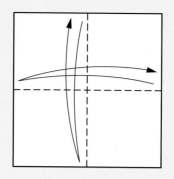

1. Fold the paper in half and unfold. Then fold the paper in half in the opposite direction and unfold. The paper is now creased into four equal sections.

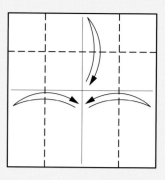

2. Fold the left, right, and top edges in to the center line. Crease, then unfold.

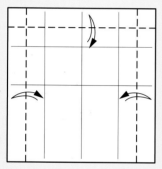

3. Repeat process, folding the edges in to the creases made in step 2.

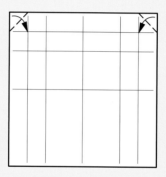

4. Fold the corners in to form triangles.

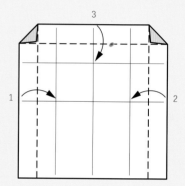

5. Fold along the existing creases following the numerical order shown above.

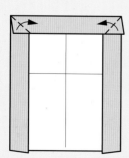

6. Fold the top corners along the dotted lines to form triangles.

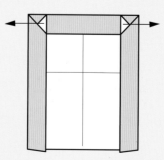

7. Pull on the colored half of each triangle to bring the inner layers out as shown in step 8.

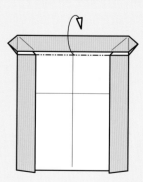

8. Fold the top back along the existing crease.

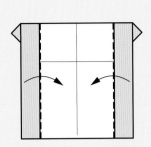

9. Fold the left and right edges in along the dotted lines.

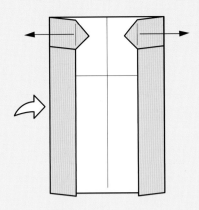

10. Pull the triangles out and flatten.

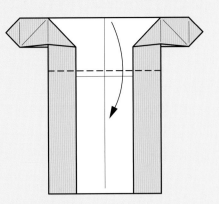

11. Fold slightly above the existing crease to bring the top edge toward the center.

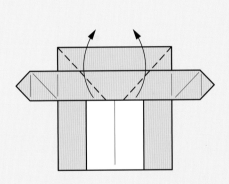

12. Fold diagonally so the ears are pointing up as shown in step 13.

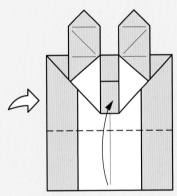

13. Fold the bottom edge up.

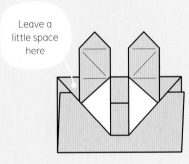

Leave a little space here

14. Completed view of step 13.

Don't forget to draw a face!

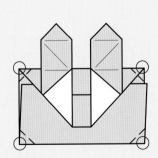

15. Fold the corners in.

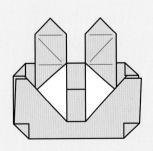

16. Completed view of step 15.

Flip over

17. The bunny is complete.

PANDA BOOKMARK

Meet your new study buddy! You'll actually look forward to homework when you have this adorable face to keep you company. The panda's arms are designed to hang over the edge of the page and act as a bookmark.

PAPER **Shape:** Square **Size:** 3 x 3in (7.5 x 7.5cm)

HOW TO MAKE

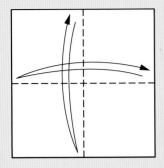

1. Fold the paper in half and unfold. Then fold the paper in half in the opposite direction and unfold. The paper is now creased into four equal sections.

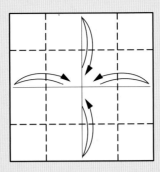

2. Fold each edge to the center, then unfold. The paper is now creased into sixteen equal sections.

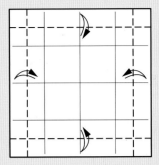

3. Follow the same process to fold each edge into the creases made in step 2. Crease, then unfold.

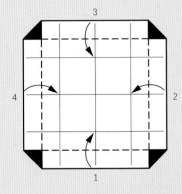

4. Fold corners in to form triangles, then fold each edge in along the existing creases following the numerical order shown above.

Look closely!

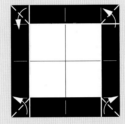

5. Fold each corner along the dotted line to form a triangle.

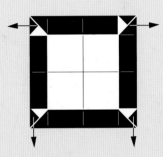

6. Pull on the colored half of each triangle to bring the inner layer out as shown in step 7.

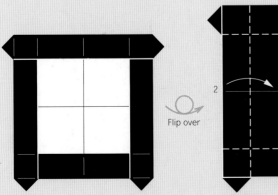

Flip over

7. Completed view of step 6.

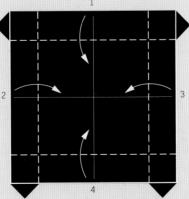

8. Fold along existing creases following the numerical order shown above.

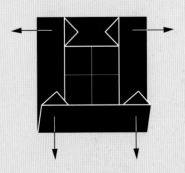

9. Pull the triangles out and flatten to form the arms and legs.

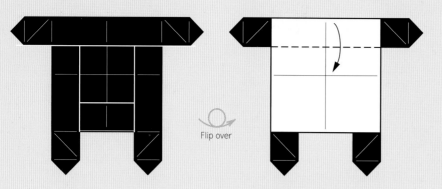

10. Completed view of step 9.

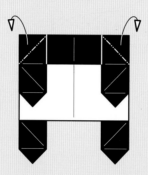

11. Fold the top down to the center.

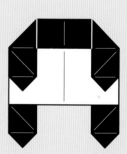

12. Fold diagonally so the arms are pointing down as shown in step 13.

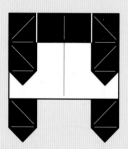

13. Completed view of step 12.

14. Fold the top corners back to form the shoulders.

15. Completed view of step 14.

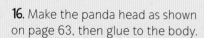

16. Make the panda head as shown on page 63, then glue to the body.

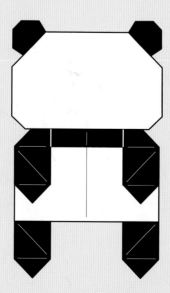

This body design works for the bunny too!

HOUSES

Have fun folding different houses and building your own village. For a festive look, position the origami paper so the right side becomes the roof. Don't forget to add doors and windows!

PAPER Shape: Square **Size:** 4 ¾–6in (11.8–15cm)

HOW TO MAKE A HOUSE WITH A FLAT ROOF

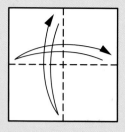

1. Fold the paper in half and unfold. Then fold the paper in half in the opposite direction and unfold. The paper is now creased into four equal sections.

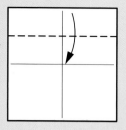

2. Fold the top edge to the center line.

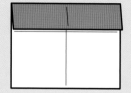

3. Completed view of step 2.

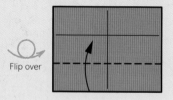

Flip over

4. Fold the bottom edge to the center line.

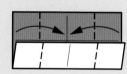

5. Fold the left and right edges to the center line.

6. Completed view of step 5.

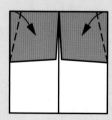

7. Fold the top corners diagonally.

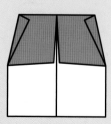

8. Completed view of step 7.

Flip over

9. The house is complete.

HOW TO MAKE A HOUSE WITH A POINTED ROOF

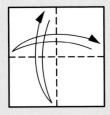

1. Fold the paper in half and unfold. Then fold the paper in half in the opposite direction and unfold. The paper is now creased into four equal sections.

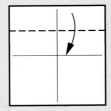

2. Fold the top edge to the center line.

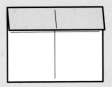

3. Completed view of step 2.

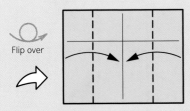

Flip over

4. Fold the left and right edges to the center line.

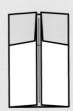

5. Completed view of step 4.

6. Fold the top corners in to the center line to create the roof.

7. Completed view of step 6.

Flip over

8. The house is complete.

If you want your message to remain hidden after folding, position the text on the top half of the paper.

ANIMAL MEMOS

These adorable little animals make excellent reminders for your desk. This project ingeniously utilizes sticky notes, so there's no need for glue or tape.

PAPER **Shape:** Rectangle or Square **Size:** 1 x 3in (2.5 x 7.5cm) or 3 x 3in (7.5 x 7.5cm)

HOW TO MAKE

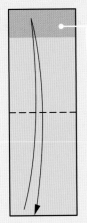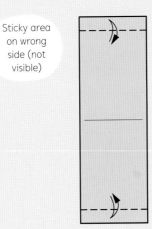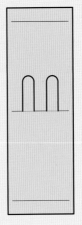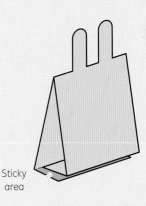

Sticky area on wrong side (not visible)

Sticky area

1. With the sticky area on the wrong side, fold in half. Crease, then unfold.

2. Fold the top and bottom edges toward the center. Crease, then unfold.

3. Use a craft knife to cut the ears along the fold. Make sure not to cut through the left and right edges of the sticky note.

4. Fold along the crease lines. Adhere the two edges using the sticky area.

Variations

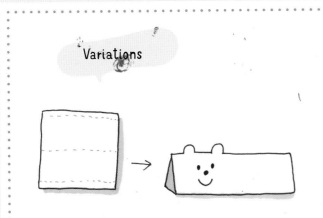

Use a square sticky note to make an oblong memo.

Bun

No need to cut, just draw the hair!

Try drawing people instead of animals.

ILLUSTRATION INSPIRATION

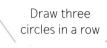

Draw three circles in a row

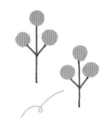

Draw a flower, then add a star at the center

Congratulations!

Draw lots of circles

Draw three circles, then add lines for stems

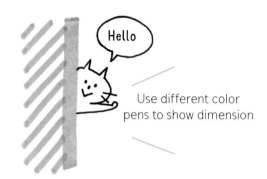
Use different color pens to show dimension

Hello

Use black pen to doodle animal faces on circles

+

Mix and match different faces and bodies to create unique characters!

Don't forget to add some accessories!

Ribbon

Crown

Glasses

Mustache

Bag

Stuffed animal

Book

Rice ball

FONT INSPIRATION

Use colored pens

Add stripes or dots

Use marker for the text, then decorate the letters with black pen

Add a speech bubble

Frame the text with a highlighter border

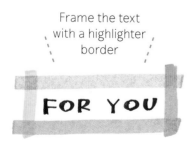

Write a letter in each square

BORDER INSPIRATION

Line + Circles

Line + Squares

Wavy Line with Two Colors

Stars + Dots

Wavy Line + Circles + Triangles

Colorful Dots

Curly Line

Repetitive Illustrations

Surround your message with circles

Let's meet at the park at 3 PM

Use part of the drawing as a frame

Coffee tomorrow?

WASHI TAPE INSPIRATION

Add tape on top of your illustration for an artistic look

Fruit

Apple

Café ☺

Tablecloth

Envelopes

Presents

For you

Houses

Flowers

Use torn pieces of tape for a natural look

Trees

NOW IT'S TIME TO PUT IT ALL TOGETHER!

Happy Birthday

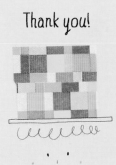

Thank you!

HELLO!

THANKS

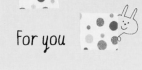

For you

Hello Origami

Published in 2017 by Zakka Workshop, a division
of World Book Media LLC
www.zakkaworkshop.com

134 Federal Street
Salem, MA 01970 USA
info@zakkaworkshop.com

ORIGAMI TEGAMI BOOK (no. 3858)
Copyright ©2014 Boutique-Sha
CHOKOTTO ORU DAKEDE KAWAII (no. 3703)
Copyright ©2013 Boutique-Sha
Originally published in Japanese language by
Boutique-Sha, Tokyo, Japan

English language rights, translation &
production by Zakka Workshop
English Editor: Lindsay Fair
Translation: Ai Jirka

ISBN: 978-1-940552-31-6

Printed in China

10 9 8 7 6 5 4 3 2 1

ABOUT THE AUTHOR

Mizutama is an illustrator and rubber stamp
artist from Japan. Her designs have been
used on a variety of stationery products,
including origami paper, sticky notes, washi
tape, and stickers. She is the author of
multiple art books in Japan.

Mizutama would like to thank Naoki
Ishibashi, who assisted with the origami
designs in this book. Naoki is a self-taught
origami artist and is the author of multiple
origami books in Japan.